We All Have

Guardian Angels

Sadie ~

May you always know
the love and protection
of your Guardian Angels.

Gina

In Memory of Canaan, our beautiful Angel.

Glory to Hosanna, for these are your words.

This book presented to:

_____

With love from:

_____

Guardian Angels are made of bright light and unconditional love. They look a lot like you with beautiful wings. They use their wings to keep up with you!

Your Guardian Angel's job is to protect you and to bring you messages from God.

They help you to make good choices and they always **Love You** no matter what.

They even love you when you make a mistake. They know that making mistakes is how you will learn to do better next time.

You can tell when your Guardian Angels are close to you because it will feel like a warm blanket and a soft hug.

You can ask your Guardian Angels to tell you their name. Just close your eyes and take deep breaths. Your Guardian Angel's name may pop into your head. You might see a sign that tells you their name, or you could even hear it.

Then the Angels will send you signs back. You will know because their messages are always good and filled with love.

Your Guardian Angels are always ready to help you whenever you need them. All you have to do is ask.

Aren't we blessed to have Guardian Angels beside us at all times to protect us and to love us?

He shall give His Angels charge over you to
keep you in all your ways. Psalm 91.11

Gina Burns has loved her Guardian Angels since childhood. So much that as a 2 year old created a hole in the stitching of her silky blanket so the Angels could sleep in the fluff at night cuddled right beside her. She also credits her Guardian Angels protective services when she was revived from drowning in a river canoeing accident at age 5.

Gina had been blessed with 5 boys of her own, one whom now flies with the Angels, 2 bonus kids and a second chance marriage to a wonderfully loving man whose unconditional love matches that of the Angels. She spent 17 years teaching first grade and earned a Masters Degree in Educational Administration and Leadership before she realized God had a greater plan. In following her passion for the Angels, she found that her mission was to share God's gift of His Angels with others.

Gina has studied under Doreen Virtue and recently took the Angel Intuitive Course with Doreen in Orange Co, CA. Gina is owner and artist of AngelArmyDecor.com. Gina enjoys teaching and speaking about the Angels she adores and encourages all of us to be the Earth Angels that God created us to be.

CPSIA information can be obtained
at www.ICGtesting.com
Printed in the USA
LVOW05s2326010716
494977LV00001B/1/P